AF270669

Pop Biographies

ZENDAYA

EMMY-WINNING ENTERTAINER

by Elizabeth Andrews

DiscoverRoo
An Imprint of Pop!
popbooksonline.com

popbooksonline.com/zendaya

abdobooks.com

Published by Pop!, a division of ABDO, PO Box 398166, Minneapolis, Minnesota 55439. Copyright © 2024 by Abdo Consulting Group, Inc. International copyrights reserved in all countries. No part of this book may be reproduced in any form without written permission from the publisher. DiscoverRoo™ is a trademark and logo of Pop!.

Printed in the United States of America, North Mankato, Minnesota.

052023
082023

Cover Photo: Getty Images
Interior Photos: Getty Images
Editor: Grace Hansen
Series Designer: Colleen McLaren

Library of Congress Control Number: 2022950557

Publisher's Cataloging-in-Publication Data
Names: Andrews, Elizabeth, author.
Title: Zendaya: emmy-winning entertainer / by Elizabeth Andrews
Other title: emmy-winning entertainer
Description: Minneapolis, Minnesota : Pop!, 2024 | Series: Pop biographies | Includes online resources and index
Identifiers: ISBN 9781098244415 (lib. bdg.) | ISBN 9781098245115 (ebook)
Subjects: LCSH: Zendaya, 1996---Juvenile literature. | Singers--Juvenile literature. | Singers--Juvenile literature. | Actresses--Juvenile literature. | Disney Channel (Firm)--Juvenile literature.
Classification: DDC 782.42166092--dc23

*Scanning QR codes requires a web-enabled smart device with a QR code reader app and a camera.

TABLE OF CONTENTS

CHAPTER 1

CALIFORNIA DREAMS

Zendaya Maree Stoermer Coleman was born September 1, 1996, in Oakland, California. She has five older half-siblings. Her parents were both teachers. Education was important to the family. Growing up, Zendaya attended different art schools.

Zendaya
started her
career as
a hip hop
dancer. But
she wouldn't
stop there!

5

Zendaya was raised in her father's childhood home. When he was growing up, the home hosted **civil rights movement** leaders who started the **Black Panther Party**. Zendaya's family were members of the party. There were civil rights meetings held in the basement of the home. Zendaya is very proud of this part of her family history.

The Black Panthers created a lot of good change for Black people in the United States.

Zendaya visits her old schools. She brings gifts and donations for the students.

As a kid, Zendaya was shy. She even had to repeat kindergarten because she didn't grow socially like her classmates. However, Zendaya was drawn to the performing arts. Her mother worked at a theater in California. Zendaya spent a lot of time there. It's where she learned to love acting.

Zendaya's family supported her dreams. They took her to dance lessons and put her in schools that gave her special opportunities. She earned roles in plays like *Richard III* and *Once on This Island*. At eight, she joined a hip-hop dance **troupe** called Future Shock.

When Zendaya was 13, her family moved to Los Angeles. Zendaya started her career by modeling for Macy's and dancing and acting in commercials. In 2009, she was the lead performer in a Kidz Bop music video for the Katy Perry Song "Hot n Cold."

Zendaya has been working since she was 13.

DISNEY DARLING

In 2009, Zendaya tried out for a role that would change her life. She danced to the Michael Jackson song "Leave Me Alone." She was cast as Rocky Blue in Disney Channel's *Shake It Up*. The show was about two teenagers from Chicago trying to become professional dancers.

Bella Thorne (left) *played CeCe opposite of Zendaya on* Shake It Up.

Shake It Up ran for three seasons

between 2010 and 2013. During this time

Zendaya released her own music. "Swag

It Out" was her first **single**. Her solo

album *Zendaya* was released in 2013. The

album's most popular song was "Replay."

Zendaya starred in the Disney Channel original movies *Frenemies* and *Zapped*. She was also a contestant on the 16th season of *Dancing with the Stars*. At just 16 years old, she was the youngest person to compete on the show! Zendaya came in second place.

Val Chmerkovskiy was Zendaya's partner on Dancing with the Stars. *The duo danced different styles, including the foxtrot and tango.*

In 2013, Zendaya and Disney began working on her second show *K.C. Undercover*. Zendaya was a **producer** for the show! She wanted the series to star a family of color. She also made sure that her character was skilled at things besides dancing and singing. She wanted young people to see that there are other things girls can be good at.

Zendaya's beautiful 2015
look went down in history!

K.C. Undercover premiered in 2015 and ran for three seasons. It starred Zendaya as Katy Cooper (K.C.), an awkward brainiac with a black belt. The show followed K.C. after she gets recruited by her super-spy parents to go on secret missions to save the world. Zendaya loved her character. She kept playing the role even after starting to act in films.

CHAPTER 3

NEW PATHS

Zendaya is grateful for her time on Disney Channel. What she learned there helped her enter the next phase of her career. In 2017, Zendaya starred as **trapeze** artist Anne Wheeler in *The Greatest Showman*. Zendaya had to become stronger for the

The toy company Mattel made a Zendaya Barbie in 2015! The doll replicates Zendaya's celebrated Academy Awards look.

role. She performed many of her own trapeze stunts. She also sang "Rewrite the Stars" for the movie.

In the same year, Zendaya played MJ in *Spider-Man: Homecoming*. This was her first film that hit theaters. People were excited to see what she had to offer. MJ is Peter Parker's smart and snarky classmate. She's different from the previous popular versions of leading ladies opposite Spider-Man.

Zendaya continued to play MJ in the last two Spider-Man installments, *Spider-Man: Far From Home* and *No Way Home*. She was 19 when the first movie came out and 25 in the final film. Zendaya says she feels like she grew up with MJ.

DID YOU KNOW?

Zendaya voices characters in cartoons. She was Chi in *Duck Duck Goose*, Meechee in *Smallfoot*, and Lola Bunny in *Space Jam: A New Legacy*.

In June 2019, Zendaya took on the role of Rue in *Euphoria*. Rue is a high school student dealing with emotional struggles. People were immediately impressed with Zendaya's skills playing a character so different from her Disney ones. Her acting in the show was called "haunting, painful, and affecting." The artistic way *Euphoria* is filmed is exciting and different.

In 2020, Zendaya won Best Actress in a TV Drama for her role as Rue. She became the youngest ever to win this Emmy award.

Season 2 of Euphoria *was released in 2022. Once again, Zendaya took home an Emmy.*

JUST GETTING STARTED

Another more serious role of Zendaya's was Marie in the 2021 movie *Malcolm & Marie.* This romantic drama was filmed during the COVID-19 pandemic. The entire crew lived and filmed in one place. They worked together in a **bubble** to stay safe and healthy.

Zendaya teamed up with Euphoria *director* Sam Levinson *to create* Malcolm & Marie.

ZENDAYA AT THE MET GALA

In 2021, the first movie in the *Dune*

series was released. Zendaya played

Chani alongside other well-known

actors. She was on screen for just seven

The Met Gala is fashion's biggest night. It is a held once a year to raise money for the Met Museum. Zendaya is known for her beautiful looks at the gala.

minutes total, but fans connected with

her character. Chani is featured more in

Dune: Part Two which came out in 2023.

Zendaya grew close with her Dune costars Jason Momoa and Timothée Chalamet.

During her career as an actor, Zendaya took on the role of **producer** as well. Producing is a big responsibility. Zendaya has overseen choosing scripts, writing, casting, and **directing**.

DID YOU KNOW? *Zendaya was a producer for K.C. Undercover, Euphoria, and Malcolm & Marie.*

Zendaya wants to use her power as a producer to make movies she wants to see. These projects would feature **diverse** people and stories. Zendaya wants to create new opportunities for the next **generation** of Black people.

MAKING CONNECTIONS

TEXT-TO-SELF

Zendaya dances, sings, and acts. What do you like to watch her do best?

TEXT-TO-TEXT

Have you read any other books about past Disney Channel stars? If so, how were they similar to or different from Zendaya?

TEXT-TO-WORLD

Some of Zendaya's family members were important to the civil rights movement. With the help of an adult, look up important people from the movement. Write a short paragraph about how they changed the world.

GLOSSARY

Black Panther Party — an organization that challenged police violence against Black people.

bubble — a group of people who only spent time together during a portion of the COVID-19 pandemic.

civil rights movement — a movement in the United States in the 1950s and 1960s. It consisted of organized efforts to end laws that involved unequal treatment of Black Americans.

direct — to carry out the organizing, energizing, and supervising of a film, play, or TV show. A person who directs is a director.

diverse — differing from one another.

generation — the entire group of people who were born around the same time.

producer — the person or company that oversees the creation of a film or TV show.

single — a song that is released as a stand-alone from an album.

trapeze — a rope swing with a bar hung high above the ground.

troupe — a group of performers.

INDEX

popbooksonline.com/zendaya

*Scanning QR codes requires a web-enabled smart device with a QR code reader app and a camera.